Wheels

Contents

Moving Around

We see wheels every day.
There are many kinds of wheels.

Ferris Wheels

Have you ever been
on a Ferris wheel?
Ferris wheels take you
high up in the air.

Skate Along

Roller skates have four wheels.
In-line skates also have four wheels,
but they are all in a line.

Sporting Wheels

Some special wheelchairs
are used for racing.
Some are used for sports,
such as tennis and basketball.

Water Wheels

Some boats have big wheels.

These boats are called paddle steamers.

The wheel turns in the water

and moves the boat along.

Floating Wheels

Some special wheels can float.
You need to pedal
if you want to move along!

Only One Wheel!

A unicycle has *one* wheel.
Riding a unicycle
takes a lot of skill!

Index